50 Things to Do Before You're 5

JOURNAL

MUST-DO **FAMILY ACTIVITIES** TO SPARK
FUN, CONNECTION, AND **CURIOSITY**

MAGGIE DOWNS

CHRONICLE BOOKS
SAN FRANCISCO

ISBN 978-1-7972-2464-0

Manufactured in China.

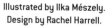

MIX
Paper from
responsible sources
FSC™ C169962
FSC www.fsc.org

Illustrated by Ilka Mészely.
Design by Rachel Harrell.

10 9 8 7 6 5 4 3 2 1

Chronicle Books publishes distinctive books and gifts. From award-winning children's titles, bestselling cookbooks, and eclectic pop culture to acclaimed works of art and design, stationery, and journals, we craft publishing that's instantly recognizable for its spirit and creativity. Enjoy our publishing and become part of our community at www.chroniclebooks.com.

Special quantity discounts are available to corporations and other organizations. Contact our premiums department at corporatesales@chroniclebooks.com or at 1-800-759-0190.

Chronicle Books LLC
680 Second Street
San Francisco, California 94107
www.chroniclebooks.com

I've spent most of my adult life in pursuit of adventure. My passion for travel has taken me rafting down the Nile River, hiking up volcanoes to encounter endangered gorillas, and trekking through ice caves. I'm an enthusiastic collector of experiences, and I'll tackle almost anything if it'll make for a great story later. I'm also a licensed skydiver—I even married my skydiving instructor, which was perhaps the biggest adventure of all.

But after my son, Everest, was born, I became rigidly attached to a daily routine. And the routine was boring. It involved lots of time in a rocking chair, many bowls of oatmeal, and never, ever leaving the house.

As a newborn, Everest was a sour, grouchy thing (imagine an eggplant that can scream), and I was exhausted, depressed, and desperate. So I figured out what worked and I stuck to it, even if it meant soothing the crying baby by marching in circles and warbling "You're a Grand Old Flag" in an oper-atic voice.

For the first time, it felt chal-lenging to leave the house at all, let alone venture to far-flung locales. I imagined being stuck in my routine forever: years of shoveling down spoonfuls of oatmeal while falling asleep at the kitchen table and singing "You're a Grand Old Flag" in my son's college dorm room.

Well-intentioned friends gave me advice: "Sleep when the baby sleeps." "Adjust your expectations." "Don't compare yourself to other parents." Most of all, they reminded me to be present with my child. "The days are long, but the years are short," they told me. "Enjoy every moment."

It's good advice, and I longed to do just that—enjoy every moment. But as a new mom, I felt more lost than ever before. It was like being given a destination but no map to get there. I grew increasingly frustrated knowing those valuable early moments were slipping away.

The idea for *50 Things to Do Before You're 5* came to me during that postpartum period. One afternoon, I remembered some-thing that had happened a couple years earlier, long before my son was born, when I attended an art gallery party. It was a flashy affair, with a slick band and pulsing lights. The dance floor was a swirl of cocktail dresses and patterned suits against a backdrop of pop art. In the midst of this kaleidoscope of color and sound, there was a man with a baby in a backpack. The baby simply observed from her perch, rapt as if the festivities were an episode of *Peppa Pig*.

"Wow, your baby is so good," I said. "I can't imagine bringing a kid to a place like this."

The man kindly but firmly corrected me and said, "My baby is good *because* we bring her to places like this."

Remembering that moment while sitting in my own living room, I realized the problem. It wasn't that I didn't want to experience life with Everest. It was that I hadn't yet imagined where we could go and what we could do. We both deserved to venture beyond the routine I had created. We had to practice being out and about.

So I started making a list. First I wrote down everything that seemed achievable at home or in our very own neighborhood. Then I pushed it further and wrote down the things that seemed more challenging or required more effort.

It worked. Once the list was compiled, it offered the guidance I needed. When I walked outside with Everest, we no longer roamed without a destination. Suddenly we had plans—planting seeds, going to the library for storytime, and seeking out tadpoles.

50 Things to Do Before You're 5 is the map I needed. It's a gentle guide designed to inspire meaningful adventures, memorable experiences, and so much fun. Think of it like a mash-up between a traditional baby book and a life to-do list. The goal is to get out of the house and into the big, beautiful world.

I've field-tested the items on this list, and the results have been nothing short of extraordinary. I have the sweetest memory of ducking into an art museum on a brutally hot day, walking Everest through the sleek, cool galleries, and showing him the paintings one by one. (He loves Rothko!) Then there was the quick weekend road trip to see the Grand Canyon and tick another national park off our list. I'll never forget how we bundled up in motel blankets at Yaki Point to watch the sunrise over the South Rim. My child actually gasped out loud as the canyons changed from deep navy to pink to brilliant gold.

Sharing these experiences as a family has unlocked the world in ways I never thought possible, and it's also sparked a sense of curiosity and wonder in my child.

As you delve into *50 Things to Do Before You're 5*, you'll discover prompts for a wide range of activities that can be done close to home with little planning, plus some aspirational items that will require more planning. Here are a few things I'd suggest you keep in mind as you make your way through these pages:

Get creative: Use this journal for guidance and inspiration, but feel free to make the activities your own, adapting them to fit your own family. Just as there isn't one right way to parent, there isn't one right way to engage with the content. This journal should be taken as a starting point rather than something to be followed to the letter.

Invest time, not money: Most of the entries in this book involve an investment of time, not cash, and are experiences designed to be accessible to everyone. Yes, seeing the Great Wall of China inspires awe but so does catching a firefly.

Be flexible: Keep in mind things will not go as planned during these activities and outings. The first time I brought Everest to a beach, I was prepared for magic. The sky was a roaring blue. Waves ebbed and flowed against soft sand and left shallow pools that were perfect for my teetering toddler to explore. Everest was delighted by the scene. He took a few running steps, then toppled face-first onto the beach. First came the sobbing, then the screaming. Everest had sand in his ears, in his mouth, in his nose, and, after rubbing his face with sandy hands, his eyes.

Strangers ran to me with water bottles and fistfuls of tissues. One person poured clean water over Everest's head until all the grime washed off. A stranger gently blew sand out of my son's eyes. Before long, Everest was running down the beach again, pausing only to dance to a nearby DJ's music.

It was not the moment I envisioned or expected. It was a different kind of magic, and it has turned into one of my favorite memories.

Adapt for various ages: These activities are designed for you to enjoy with children from infants to five-year-olds, but don't feel rushed to complete these experiences. There is no deadline. For younger children, the goal is to get outside the house and interact with the world, exposing them to new sights, sounds, and sensations. For children between two and five, it's about deepening your bond, fostering connection with your community, and making meaningful memories.

Have fun! As you're making your own memories with *50 Things to Do Before You're 5*, the most important thing to remember is to have fun. I know this firsthand. As much as I love traveling solo, there is a richness and deep pleasure to be found by soaking in the world with the people you love. That's what I want for your family too.

—Maggie Downs

Attend a storytime

Being read to is a lovely experience, for both children and adults. Listening to stories helps cultivate a love of books, discover language, learn about story structure, and build imagination. It's also a nice opportunity to interact with other families and members of your community.

You can often find storytime programs at a local library, bookstore, or community center. You could also consider gathering some friends and hosting your own storytime. You can even attend storytimes when you're traveling away from home—it's a great way to connect with a new place and feel like part of a community.

When story hour is over, spend some time connecting with one another about the experience—including favorite parts or characters, any surprises in the book, and how the narrator brought the story to life through voices, gestures, or other devices.

What happened during storytime?

DATE:

LOCATION:

PARTICIPANTS:

Have a picnic

Avoid the hustle and bustle of a busy restaurant by packing your own to-go meal for a relaxing family-friendly picnic.

A picnic can take place almost anywhere—a remote beach, a cute corner in your local park, a bench over-looking a lake. Simply pack some utensils, napkins, and favorite foods (aim for goodies that don't involve too much fuss or mess), and you're ready to go!

This is a really fun activity to do with friends, so the more the merrier. Pack food to share; bring along some portable games, like a Frisbee or soccer ball; and enjoy this alfresco dining experience. This is also an easy activity to do with babies—bring a blanket for tummy time and a stroller or sun tent for shade.

Reflect on your family picnic:

DATE:

LOCATION:

PARTICIPANTS:

Take a smell walk

There's a reason people always say to stop and smell the roses. Slowing down and focusing on your sense of smell open up a new way of experiencing the world. And research shows that scent-based memories are more vivid and smell has a stronger link to emotion than other senses—so the citrus blossoms, freshly cut grass, or the just-baked cookies that you and your child smell today could form a lifetime of lasting memories.

Take a stroll near your home, and focus your attention on the scents of your neighborhood. Can you smell somebody baking? Or doing laundry? Maybe there's a factory nearby. Help your child identify what might be new smells to them. What do the aromas reveal about the place where you live?

Even newborns have a developed sense of smell that only grows stronger as they do, though this experience will become more engaging as your child gets older.

Pay special attention to how your smellscape might differ from your child's perspective. Fragrance researchers have found that the world can smell very different at a child's height!

Reflect on your smell walk:

DATE:

LOCATION:

PARTICIPANTS:

Visit an art museum

Art is eye candy for infants and small children. Just think of all the visual confections: The colors! The shapes! Faces and places and patterns! Museums are a delight for other senses too. Some museums have interactive exhibits that allow your little one to touch (and sometimes hear or smell!) the art sparking imagination and providing a foundation for their own creativity.

For older children, ask them about their favorite pieces of artwork, favorite artists, or favorite areas of the museum. Young babies can also experience the wonders of an art museum. While newborns see mostly in black and white, babies' vision changes rapidly. Around one month, an infant can see the brightness of colors, and by four months, color vision is fully developed. The bold images, depictions of humans and animals, and dynamic scenes found at a museum can stimulate a child's sight and help them interpret their surroundings.

What happened on the visit to the museum?

DATE:

LOCATION:

PARTICIPANTS:

Spend time in a garden

Spending time in a garden brings an abundance of sweet surprises. You can talk about how plants grow, point out different colors and textures, notice the weather, and see if you can spot any bugs, birds, or other wildlife.

If you have the space and time, consider planting your own small garden, which brings a wide range of benefits, since plants aren't the only things that grow in a garden—your little one's mind can grow as well. Gardening activities—like planting seeds, watering flowers, and digging in the dirt—can boost children's brains with math and science concepts, sensory exploration, and motor-skill development.

Creating your own small garden has other bonuses too. Plants gulp down the carbon dioxide in the air and release oxygen, improving air quality in your neighborhood. Gardens can also attract pollinators to your area, which are a vital part of a healthy ecosystem.

If you don't have space for a garden bed, try a hanging pot, wall-mounted garden, or window box instead. You could also spend time at a local community garden or consider sharing plants with a neighbor who does have space. And part of the fun of gardening is sampling what you've grown, whether you take a bite of a recently-picked vegetable, use fresh herbs for cooking, or cut some blooms to beautify your home.

Write about your time in the garden:

DATE:

LOCATION:

PARTICIPANTS:

BEFORE YOU'RE 5

Interact with a bug or worm

Bugs like beetles, ladybugs, crickets, and grasshoppers can be perfect pals for curious children. Bugs are also an excellent entry point to help kids get excited about nature. The goal here is to have some kind of interaction with an insect, whether that means following a line of ants, gazing at a ladybug, or holding an earthworm. Depending on where you live, maybe you could also catch and release a firefly or take a walk through a butterfly house.

You can find bugs almost everywhere—in your local park, in your backyard, or on the sidewalk outside your home. Always take care that the insect is safe and won't bite or sting. In general, most ground beetles, ladybugs, crickets, grasshoppers, and rolypolies are safe to interact with. (Technically rolypolies aren't bugs, they're terrestrial crustaceans, but they're great too!) Of course, take great care not to harm the insect during your interaction.

Spend some time observing the insect together and talking about it in as much detail as possible. Follow it if you can. Talk about where it might live, how it spends its days, and what it eats. You might have an older child try and sketch the bug or have them describe it to you so that you can sketch it.

What was it like to interact with a bug?

DATE:

LOCATION:

PARTICIPANTS:

Talk to an older person

DATE:

LOCATION:

PARTICIPANTS:

There is so much to learn simply by having a conversation with someone who has more lived experience. That's why talking to an older adult can be a special activity. Find a relative, a neighbor, or a trusted person in your community, and see what they have to share. Maybe you'll make a valuable new connection!

Ask them about their childhood, where they live, their first job, and any major world events they lived through. Keep in mind that intergenerational relationships can be enriching on both sides. The older person learns from the younger one, and the younger one gains perspective and knowledge from the older adult. It's also fun to compare the differences and similarities between generations.

What did you talk about? Was the conversation funny, challenging, easy, or interesting? What's one thing that was learned through this experience?

Reflect on your conversation:

Dress up like a character from a favorite story

Of course, you already know your child is a character. Now it's time to don a costume and show the world—or, at least, your household—how much they really are.

For this task, have a dress-up day with your family, choosing a beloved character or superhero from a favorite book. Why? Pretending to be another person is fun. It gives us the ability to temporarily try on character traits along with the costume. This is especially helpful to do when spirits are low—dressing up and playing a role can help us feel more powerful and confident.

One study researched this phenomenon, what they called the "Batman effect," and found that kids who wear costumes work harder and focus more on their tasks.

It doesn't have to be anything fancy. A pajama onesie and a construction paper crown can instantly turn a child into Max from *Where the Wild Things Are*, while a sheet tied like a cape can transform a parent into a young wizard. Or maybe this is an opportunity to create a new fantasy character that nobody has ever heard of before.

Reflect on the experience of being in character:

DATE:

LOCATION:

PARTICIPANTS:

BEFORE YOU'RE 5

Tour a state or national park

Public lands like state and national parks offer many opportunities for exploration. Visiting a park with kids is the perfect way to go on an outdoor adventure, see magnificent landscapes, experience the solitude of the wilderness, and learn about plants and animals.

You don't have to be a serious outdoors person to enjoy a state park or national park. Parks offer a wide range of activities for any level of outdoor comfort—you could bring a picnic, take a short hike, dip your toes in a lake, or take a guided shuttle tour. And visiting a park doesn't have to be a multi-day undertaking. Most people in the United States live within one hour or so of a national park, and there are more than 6,600 state parks across the country. Check out a map and find a park close to you!

When you arrive, stop by the ranger station or visitor's center. Many parks offer junior ranger programs or kid-friendly activities, like storytime, accessible recreational trails, guided walks, and more. Pick up a map while you're there, and ask about important safety advice to ensure a fun and safe visit.

What happened on your visit to the park?

DATE:

LOCATION:

PARTICIPANTS:

Build a collection

A collection is simply an assortment of objects, which means the sky's the limit with this activity! You can make a collection out of anything that piques your child's interest: snow globes, stickers, leaves, toy cars, stamps, souvenir pressed pennies, unusual rocks—truly anything.

Building a collection helps us appreciate beautiful and interesting things. It's a chance to learn something new or connect with the past. It also gives us a way to bond with others who share this interest, whether you're seeking out items at a flea market, picking up a special souvenir on vacation, or looking for unusual rocks around your neighborhood.

Let your child's interest guide this activity—follow their lead and let them help decide what kind of collection they'd like to start. You can talk about how they plan to store the collection and how they hope to add to the collection. Are there any hard-to-find objects they hope to add? You could also have fun together creating a box, book, or shelf to showcase the growing collection.

Write about the collection you've built:

DATE:

LOCATION:

PARTICIPANTS:

Watch the sunrise

Greet the new day by watching the sunrise! Making the conscious decision to watch the sun make its way through the morning sky with your child is something special. Beginning your day with the sunrise injects beauty into the day, it shows us the wonder of nature, and it offers a moment of stillness, a chance to be present before the commotion of everyday life.

You can watch the sunrise from a dramatic look-out point, from your kitchen window, or from the sidewalk outside your home. What's important is that you're spending time together under a radiant sky, transforming an ordinary morning into the extraordinary.

Depending on your child's age, this can also be a great chance to start talking about scientific concepts, like the rotation of the Earth, our atmosphere, and how light creates colors in the sky. You can also play a game of naming all the colors you see in the sky at sunrise.

Reflect on watching the sunrise:

DATE:

LOCATION:

PARTICIPANTS:

Find creatures in the water

Uncover a whole new world by searching for creatures that live in the water.

Along rocky coasts you can discover tide pools, the shallow pools that remain after the tide recedes. (Check your local tide report to find the best time for low tide.) These tiny pools can be bountiful with life, including snails, sea urchins, barnacles, anemones, crustaceans, and fish. You might also spy beautiful rocks, delicate coral, and plant life. What kind of colors can you find? What textures can you feel? Discuss how some creatures blend in with their surroundings.

For those who don't live near the ocean, seek out tadpoles, a fascinating way to see science in action. They are typically found during spring and summer in small bodies of water, including ponds, lakes, streams, rivers, and wetlands all over the world. (But not Antarctica!) You can typically spot them along the edges, where the water is shallow and calm, since frogs tend to lay eggs where the water will dry up over time, protecting the tadpoles from predator fish. You can find tadpoles in various states of transformation, from clear eggs with black dots to bigger pollywogs with legs emerging.

(Some places have restrictions on collecting amphibians, so make sure you're familiar with local rules, and always leave the tadpoles where you found them.)

What happened on your creature-seeking adventure?

DATE:

LOCATION:

PARTICIPANTS:

BEFORE YOU'RE 5

Attend a carnival or festival

Going to a carnival or festival is a fun way to strengthen communication between adults and children as you discuss what you're going to see, make decisions about what to do, and talk about the pageantry happening all around. These events also encourage self-expression and inspire interaction with a varied group of people. This could be anything from an epic event like a multi-day music festival or a hometown fair in a parking lot.

With a variety of booths and activities to choose from, this is a good way for the whole family to try something new and offers endless sensory experiences. Engage with the people around you. Check out a new band. Play a game. Sample a food you've never tasted before. Dance with joy.

Reflect on attending the event:

DATE:

LOCATION:

PARTICIPANTS:

Visit a factory

Go behind the scenes for a unique experience to see how things are made. Taking a tour of a factory is a chance to see a product go from raw materials to the packaged product. It's cool to see where things come from and how much work, skill, and artistry is involved. You'll leave with a greater appreciation for objects you might not have noticed before.

For very young children, this is a chance to expose them to new sensory delights, while older children will get a behind-the-scenes look at everyday items and a memorable lesson in engineering and design.

There are factory tours for everyone's interests, from cheese to crayons to baseball bats. See where your curiosity will take you! Tours of candy factories can be particularly interesting and colorful—you should see how jellybeans are made—and some confectioners even give you the opportunity to make your own chocolate bars or truffles.

After the visit, you can chat about what each person found to be the most interesting part of the process or have your child draw something they observed, like a product or machine.

Use the space below to jot down a few notes about the experience, and use the blank page opposite to draw something you observed on your visit.

DATE:

LOCATION:

PARTICIPANTS:

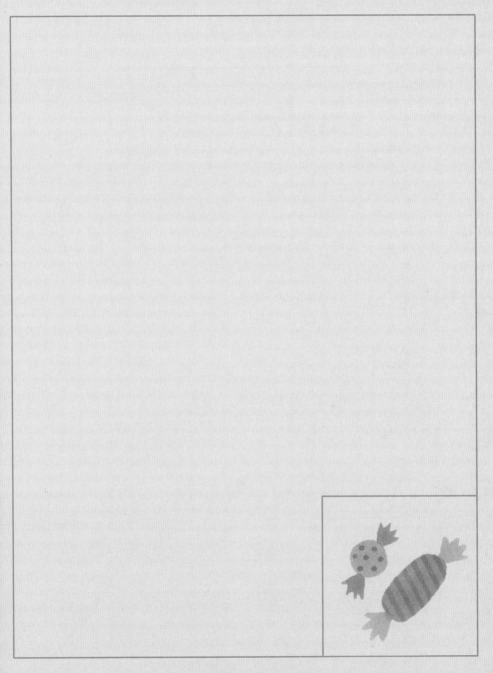

BEFORE YOU'RE 5

Pose for a portrait

Take turns drawing portraits of one another as a family. Any materials work—watercolors, crayons, pastels, colored pencils. Or you could cut out pieces of magazines and colored paper to create a collage. Get creative with it!

Making portraits encourages focus and creativity, and the result allows us to see ourselves through someone else's eyes. Very little ones might make scribble drawings, while older children might be able to experiment with scale, accuracy, and color.

It's a valuable experience to spend time focusing on the other people in your household and truly looking at them. When was the last time you actually spent time gazing at your loved ones' faces? Talk about what you each noticed during the experience— maybe you noticed something for the very first time.

Use the space below to jot down a few notes about the experience, and use the blank page opposite for your portrait sketch.

DATE:

LOCATION:

PARTICIPANTS:

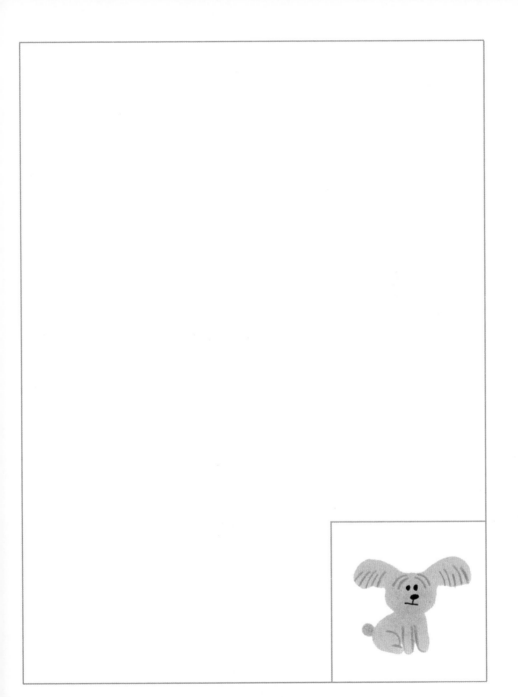

BEFORE YOU'RE 5

Gaze at the night sky

Introduce your little one to the wonders of the universe by gazing at the night sky. This is something that can be done almost anywhere on a clear night, but the farther away you are from artificial light the better.

A full moon is something that even very young children can observe. Look up the date of the next full moon, and make a plan to see it together. Look toward the east to see the moon rising and west to see the sun setting.

With toddlers and older children, you can try to find constellations, like Orion's Belt, the Big Dipper, and Little Dipper, or look for shooting stars. You can also look up astrological events like meteor showers or lunar eclipses. Gazing at the night sky is also a wonderful opportunity to begin to talk about space exploration, planets, and solar systems.

Reflect on gazing at the night sky:

DATE:

LOCATION:

PARTICIPANTS:

Celebrate autumn with leaves

Get some fresh air, burn off some energy, and build core memories during this outdoor activity. All you have to do is find some leaves, pile them up, and have loads of silly fun.

This activity can be done anywhere that's rich with fallen leaves, whether it's your own yard or a public park. First walk around the area and make sure there aren't any sticks, rocks, or objects that might injure anyone while jumping. Then gather up some leaves—it's extra fun when your child helps—and launch yourselves into the pile! Don't stop until you can't catch your breath from laughing too much.

If finding a pile of leaves is challenging where you live, go for a walk and gather leaves for a leaf collection instead. See what kind of shapes, textures and colors you can find. Maybe you can turn these into an art project with your child: Press them into a leaf book, draw on the leaves with markers or glitter glue, or paste them onto paper and make a leaf collage. Let your child crunch and tear them too!

Think about how leaves might signal autumn for your family. What did they smell like? How did they sound? What colors did you see?

Reflect on how you celebrated autumn:

DATE:

LOCATION:

PARTICIPANTS:

BEFORE YOU'RE 5

Build a snowman

Bundle up for some winter fun and build a snowman! This activity gets the family working together to create a work of snow art.

The traditional snowman is constructed from three round snowballs stacked on top of each other—the largest one on the bottom, and the smallest one on top. But you don't have to limit yourself to snowmen. You could build snow kids, snow aliens, or snow squid! Let the creative ideas flow as you pack the snow together, including everyone in the creation process. Very young children can engage in this experience by touching snow for the first time or trying to throw a small snowball, while older kids can engage by conceptualizing the creature, packing the snow, and finding materials to create arms, faces, and more.

If finding snow is out of the question, see what kind of snowman you can build with craft supplies or items around the house. What can your child find to build their own version of Frosty? Maybe a stack of books with white jackets, painted jars and buckets, fabric, styrofoam, cotton balls?

Use the space below to jot down a few notes about the experience, and use the blank page opposite to draw your snow creation.

DATE:

LOCATION:

PARTICIPANTS:

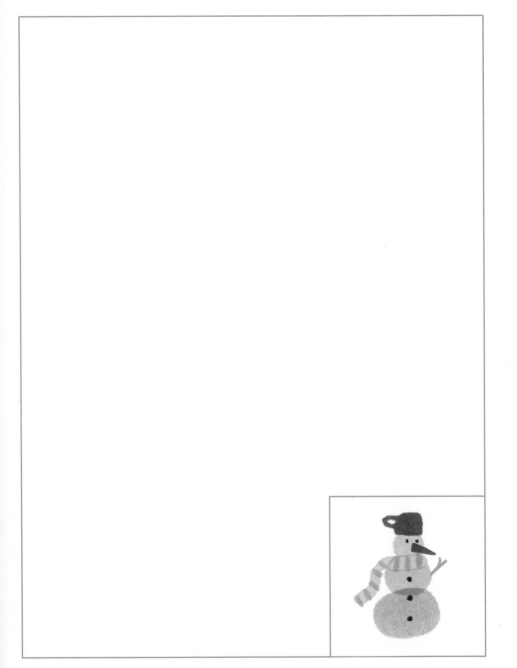

Ride a horse

Horses are amazing animals with sleek bodies, gentle dispositions, and large, warm eyes. Many children are immediately drawn to them, and a first encounter with a horse can be a special occasion, whether it's petting a pony at the local fair or riding a horse at an equestrian center.

Riding is good for developing balance and coordination, improving flexibility, and getting little muscles moving. But even better is the emotional connection that is established. Horses and humans often share a powerful connection, which leaves a lasting and profound effect.

With proper supervision, children as young as two to three years old can ride a smaller horse or pony, though this varies depending on the farm or stable. It's best to check in advance if you're unsure. If riding isn't in the cards, or your child is too young to ride, you can interact with horses by petting or brushing them or offering them snacks like carrots and apples (of course, check with the farm or stable staff first!).

What was it like to spend time with a horse?

DATE:

LOCATION:

PARTICIPANTS:

BEFORE YOU'RE 5

Take pictures together in a photo booth

They say a picture is worth a thousand words, but somehow photos of our kids feel like they're worth many times that. That's exactly why you should take advantage of photo booths—the big machines that spit out strips of images—and stick the photos in your family album, hang them on the fridge, or tape them inside this book!

You'll find photo booths in public places like malls, hotels, restaurants, amusement parks, or at wedding receptions. Basically, anywhere there's a crowd ready to have a good time.

Hop inside the booth with whomever you're with, then strike funny poses or try different facial expressions—blow kisses at the camera, get extremely close to the camera, pout, make a heart with your hands, stick your tongue out, make your silliest face. The possibilities are endless, and the results are priceless.

What was your experience in a photo booth?

PHOTO

BEFORE YOU'RE 5

Hunt for a rainbow

Rainbows are magical displays that can inspire feelings of wonder in all who view them. Your best chance of finding a rainbow is to make a point of looking at the sky, in the opposite direction of the sun, after it rains.

If you aren't able to spot a rainbow, you can still hunt for rainbow colors. Stroll or take a leisurely drive through the most colorful place near where you live. Look for each of the colors of the rainbow (red, orange, yellow, green, blue, indigo, and violet) and call them out one by one.

If you want to make your rainbow hunt more challenging, come up with a theme. For example, you could try to find flowers, signs, vehicles, or buildings in each color of the rainbow.

What did you discover on your rainbow hunt?

DATE:

LOCATION:

PARTICIPANTS:

Play in the rain

Here's the silver lining of wet days: Rainy weather can make for such fun play! Rain offers a completely new and different sensory experience for children, providing new surfaces like mud, puddles, and wet grass to test balance and motor skills. Plus, everything feels, smells, sounds, and looks different in the rain.

Take a stroll through your neighborhood or venture out into your yard and notice how the world is changed by rain. What happens to plants and flowers? Is anything muddy? What does the sky look like? Best of all, what happens when you jump into a puddle?

Of course, the conditions have to be right for rainy-day adventures. High winds, flash floods, and storms with lightning could be dangerous, so use caution when venturing out in wet weather. And once playtime is over, make sure to towel off and put on dry clothes as soon as possible.

What was it like to play in the rain?

DATE:

LOCATION:

PARTICIPANTS:

Visit the local library

A library card is so much more than just a tool for checking out books. A library card unlocks all sorts of entertainment and activity. Librarians are wonderful resources for information and, depending on where you live, your library might lend movies, state park passes, tools, bicycles, or even board games!

Having a library card of their own can be such a source of pride for a child, and using it teaches responsibility, offers a sense of independence, and opens up the world. Keep in mind some libraries require that a child must be able to print their own name in order to get a card. If that's the case, this is something to work toward! Make it a celebration when the child hits this milestone and receives their own card.

And don't be afraid to take a young child to the library even before they are ready for their own card. Libraries are shared neighborhood spaces open to all—that includes younger kids. Spending time there with a child is an excellent way to build a lifelong love for reading, learning, and community.

Reflect on your visit to the library:

DATE:

LOCATION:

PARTICIPANTS:

BEFORE YOU'RE 5

Play a musical instrument

Children can enjoy music from infancy, and both listening to and playing music is an important part of early childhood development. Numerous studies have shown that exposure to sound and rhythm stimulates neural pathways, while playing an instrument helps the body and mind learn to work together.

Some good instruments to introduce at a young age include harmonicas, recorders, ukuleles (or guitars built for little hands), and almost anything percussive, like drums, bongos, tambourines, and maracas. Pass the instruments around and see what music your child responds to and what they enjoy playing.

What happened during your music session?

DATE:

LOCATION:

PARTICIPANTS:

Write a book

Storytelling allows a child's imagination to soar. Encouraging a child to come up with their own story allows them to express their unique voice and ignites self-discovery. It also offers insight into their thoughts and feelings. And sitting down to put their stories to paper reinforces the message that their stories are valuable.

To write a storybook together, sit down with a small stack of blank paper or a blank notebook and some fun writing supplies, like colored pencils or glitter pens. Then offer some prompts to get ideas flowing: Ask for a story about a favorite stuffed animal. Look at a painting or photograph and tell a story about what's happening there. Talk about a beloved book and see if there's a way to retell that story.

Now write the story down together! Perhaps your story is complete in one go, or maybe you can add chapters as time goes by.

What was it like writing a book together?

DATE:

LOCATION:

PARTICIPANTS:

Go to the movies

Lights, camera, popcorn! It's time to go to the movies. Going out to a film together can make for a special shared experience. And there are many options for how to watch a movie on the big screen. You could go to a drive-in, a local cinema, or a screening at the library; some places even hold screenings at local parks or neighborhood swimming pools. Consider what type of viewing experience your child would like best, and pick an age-appropriate film. After the movie ends, talk about your favorite parts—characters, songs, and scenes.

Note: This activity is for children older than age two. Many experts recommend that babies under twenty-four months should not go to the movies due to the noise level and large screen. However, some movie theaters or community centers have special screenings for parents with babies in which the volume is lowered and screens are dimmed, with changing stations in the aisles.

Reflect on your experience going to the movies:

Sing together

Belting out tunes is a surefire mood booster! Pick one of your child's favorite jams and sing it together, loud and proud. Singing does so much for children of all ages; it develops memory, offers a chance to be vocal, cultivates communication skills, and releases endorphins.

Will you be singing in front of others? Participating in a sing-along tune is always a crowd-pleaser, whether it's a kid's song or a selection from a popular musical. Or maybe this is something you'll do privately at home, which is fun too! Discuss what kind of songs you enjoy, listen to some tunes together, and see which ones cultivate the most joy in your child.

With older children, you might try writing a song together, which is an excellent way to work vocabulary skills and practice rhyming. You can even change the lyrics to a song you already love.

What was it like to sing together? What did you sing?

DATE:

LOCATION:

PARTICIPANTS:

Go for a hike

DATE:

LOCATION:

PARTICIPANTS:

The great outdoors offers endless opportunities for exploration with kids! When your baby has enough head and neck control for a carrier (usually between three and six months, but check with your pediatrician), you can take a hike! This experience is a breath of fresh air, literally, and simply spending time outdoors in nature can bring about a sense of accomplishment.

Hiking with children doesn't always go as planned, so be flexible, and keep in mind that this experience isn't about summiting a mountain or making it to the end of a trail. The journey is the destination! Don't forget to pack plenty of snacks, water, and extras of anything else you might need, like wipes or diapers.

Write down which trail you took and interesting things you noticed along the way.

What was the hike like?

Wade into a large body of water

DATE:

LOCATION:

PARTICIPANTS:

It's time to go with the flow! Let your little one experience a large body of water, like a lake, river, or ocean. This activity offers so many sensory experiences—the temperature of the water, the feeling of the sand beneath their feet, the sensation of the current or waves.

Choose a calm spot that's shallow enough to keep a firm footing. Stay within arm's reach at all times. And if there's a swift current, don't go in the water. Remember this adventure isn't about swimming, it's about exploring the sensation of being in water; non-swimmers should remain in shallow water where they can stand with their head above the surface.

While there's no official recommendation for the age at which a child can take this kind of dip, many experts say to wait until six months or older, as newborns have trouble regulating their body temperature and need a more mature immune system for any bacteria they might encounter.

Write about your experience in water:

Bake cookies

Spending time in the kitchen with your child is a wonderful way to begin to teach them about food, flavors, kitchen tools, measurements, and the rewards of patience.

For this activity, pick an easy cookie recipe and involve your child in the baking process. Children as young as eighteen months can help out with baking, as long as they are supervised and have a safe area designated for them (make sure no sharp knives, scissors, or other dangerous implements are within reach). You can task them with spooning ingredients into measuring cups, pouring the ingredients into the bowl, mixing the batter, or placing the cookies onto baking sheets. Yes, things will probably get messy—but that's part of the fun!

Afterward, enjoy the cookies together and talk about your favorite parts of the process. You can also bring your cookies to friends, neighbors, or relatives—sharing the experience with loved ones will make it even sweeter.

Write about your experience baking together:

DATE:

LOCATION:

PARTICIPANTS:

Cross a border

Traveling with children is a wonderful way to give them new perspectives, both on their home and on new places. While traveling with children might not always be a breeze, kids are naturally adaptable and inquisitive. Travel builds empathy, cultivates curiosity, and helps expose children to different foods and traditions. Being in new places also offers opportunities to talk about history and geography and ignites a sense of adventure.

For this experience, travel across a border, any border— it could mean the border of your town, your county, your state, or your country. Once you've crossed the border, pick at least one thing to do on the other side before you return home: eat a meal, visit a park, see live music, visit a market. For babies, the experience of new sights, sounds, flavors, and smells will be wonderful and stimulating and help them become adaptable little adventurers. With older kids, talk to them about the differences and similarities they notice between your home and the place you're visiting.

Write about your travel experience:

DATE:

LOCATION:

PARTICIPANTS:

BEFORE YOU'RE 5

Take a road trip

Being in the car together for an extended time offers a bonding experience like no other. Road trips are a great time to catch up, ask questions, play games, and share stories while leaving the ordinary world behind.

Pick a destination—maybe it's a visit to a loved one, a vacation rental, or a national park—and plot out fun places to take breaks along the way. For some, this might be a daylong road trip, while others might want to tackle a more ambitious, multiday trip. Know that things might not go according to plan. Road trips, by nature, offer a chance to be flexible and have spontaneous adventures. It's all part of the experience.

A road trip also gives you insight into how your family likes to travel: Do you prefer the highways or the slower scenic route? Will you stop at notable landmarks or quirky roadside attractions?

Where did you go on your road trip, and what happened along the way?

DATE:

LOCATION:

PARTICIPANTS:

BEFORE YOU'RE 5

Attend a sports game

Bonding over favorite teams is a fun way to engage young children, and there's nothing quite like attending a professional sports game. Even if you're not particularly into sports, it's easy to get caught up in the excitement of the crowd and cheer for a team. The air crackles with energy, and there's music, bright lights, color everywhere, and delicious snacks galore. After the game, you can rehash the exciting moments, talk about favorite players, or even re-create favorite plays.

If a major league sports event isn't accessible, look for a minor league game, a rousing college match, or a local team you haven't seen before.

Crowds and stadium noise might be too loud for a young child's ears, especially if the game is indoors. Consider using noise-limiting headphones to help protect their hearing while still having fun.

Write about your experience at the event:

Eat something that's been set on fire

Flambé dishes, which involve using a burst of flame to cook ingredients, are always kid-pleasers! (But maybe don't try this one at home, unless you are already skilled in the culinary arts.) Watching food be set on fire is exhilarating, and it's a great opportunity to talk about how heat can transform ingredients.

Do a little research to find a local restaurant with flambé items on their menu. Flambé dishes include bananas foster, bombe Alaska, cherries jubilee, and crêpes suzette. If you're hard-pressed to find a place that does flambéing, crème brûlée (which is made with a culinary blowtorch) or roasted marshmallows could also do in a pinch.

What was your flambé experience?

Attend a parade

Watching a parade is a special activity for a child. The music, festive costumes, dancers, and colorful floats can ignite a sense of wonder. Pick a spot with a good view, and bring supplies—such as chairs, a stroller, snacks, and drinks—so that you can comfortably enjoy the spectacle.

If you're feeling more ambitious, consider participating in the parade by riding on a float or marching. The good news is that you don't have to hold a balloon in the Macy's Thanksgiving Day Parade to join a parade. (Although that would be very memorable too!) You can march in a parade within your own community by participating with a volunteer group, pushing a stroller alongside a local official, or joining a local band, dance group, or float.

What was it like to attend a parade?

DATE:

LOCATION:

PARTICIPANTS:

BEFORE YOU'RE 5

Visit a fire truck

They're shiny, they're bright red, and they have lights and sirens. No wonder fire trucks are all the rage among children.

To get an up close look at a ladder, truck, or engine, call your local fire department and set up a time to stop by. Sometimes fire departments also visit schools or community festivals.

In addition to learning basic fire safety, your child can also become acquainted with firefighters, their gear, and everything that happens at a fire department.

There's so much to discover! Find out how fire hydrants work. Check out all the different types of hoses and how they are used on fires. See what firefighters wear while battling blazes. Learn how firefighters stay healthy, and find out how they respond quickly when there's an emergency.

Fire trucks are fascinating because they're huge and contain so many parts—ladders, hoses, lights, and more. And a fire engine also contains other tools used by firefighters, like hammers, axes, and chainsaws. It's a great opportunity to talk about tools and how they're used to help people and fight fires.

What was it like to get close to a fire truck and meet firefighters?

DATE:

LOCATION:

PARTICIPANTS:

Make a wish on a dandelion

Making a wish unleashes a child's imagination. It allows them to think about the future. It teaches them about hope. For younger children, it can also be an opportunity to learn how to use their breath.

To make a dandelion wish, you'll need dandelions, after the flowers have turned into white globes of exposed seeds. (They look like puffballs!) Each person should hold a flower, think about their wish, take a deep breath, and blow until the seeds scatter. You can watch the wind carry the seeds and talk about where the seeds might go and how they might turn into their own flowers one day.

If your child is old enough to speak and is comfortable sharing their wishes, they can include them on the page below. Or maybe you have a few of your own to share.

Write about your dandelion wish experience:

Fly

Journey into the wild blue yonder on a real flying machine! Children of any age can fly on airplanes, but older kiddos can enjoy other types of flights too, including helicopters, ultralights, and hot-air balloons (these can often be booked during air shows or festivals).

Flight offers a profound shift in perspective by witnessing the magnitude of the earth from a bird's-eye view and discovering how small we are in it. But it also unleashes the sky and all the freedom that comes from soaring as high as the clouds.

You can also explore the sensation of flying with your child, like you would on an amusement park ride or even playground swings. Discuss what makes flying an exhilarating experience. Ask them to describe the sensation in their own words. (If they didn't enjoy it, that's something to discuss too!) For older kids, you can make scientific observations about the flight, like asking what they felt? What did they hear? Did their ears pop? What else did they notice?

Reflect on your flying experience:

DATE:

LOCATION:

PARTICIPANTS:

Attend a ballet, opera, or symphony

Don some dress-up duds and attend a performance, like the opera, ballet, symphony, or play.

This comes with some surprising benefits for children. Researchers have found that viewing live productions increases vocabulary, inspires tolerance, and improves a child's ability to read the emotions of others. This cultural consumption offers a safe space for children to spend time seeing the world through a character's eyes, like during a play, or building empathy for performers. Watching a production is also an act of mindfulness, an opportunity to slow down and learn patience.

Many event spaces offer family-friendly programs, with shorter performances, interactive games, and hands-on musical activities to engage young audiences.

If the program you attend isn't designed for families, you can still make it an educational experience by looking online for information about the performance you're attending and learning about the composer, the orchestra, or the conductor.

Afterward, have a discussion about what your child enjoyed most about the program.

Write about the experience of going to a performance:

DATE:

LOCATION:

PARTICIPANTS:

Paddle a boat

This experience is quite an *oar* deal! Paddling a boat, kayak, or canoe helps children get comfortable with water and cultivates an appreciation for nature. The gentle lapping of the water is soothing, while spending time watching birds, marine mammals, fish, frogs, and other wildlife is a wonderful way to learn about aquatic ecosystems. Spending time in the natural world has been proven to have all sorts of physical, mental, and emotional benefits, and you can help your child foster a love of nature from an early age.

Many paddling centers offer child-sized paddles and cushions to sit on for their comfort in a boat. While paddling, children will discover the joy of self-powered transportation and learn about cause and effect as they learn what the paddle can do to move the boat forward, backward, or sideways, all while enjoying valuable time outdoors.

Be sure to pick a calm area with flat water, like a pond or small lake, for this activity, and check the weather so that you're not in for any unpleasant surprises while you're out on the open water. For safety, always make sure your child is wearing a floatation device and is supervised.

What happened on your paddling adventure?

Climb a tree

Climbing a tree is an adventure, a chance to explore the world from a different perspective. Tree branches can fire up a child's imagination and provide an entryway into endless fairytale realms. Not to mention, the act of climbing also strengthens a child's physical skills, like balance, agility, and hand-foot coordination.

This activity is a playful challenge, offering a chance to take calculated risks while developing self-confidence and having fun. Start with smaller trees so that children can build their climbing skills safely. Always be sure to pick a tree with strong limbs, and spot your child as they climb.

Younger children who aren't yet ready to climb can still interact with a tree. Let them toddle up to the trunk and explore the bark and roots (if any are within sight). Lift them up to examine the branches and leaves. Allow them to touch, see, and smell the tree.

Notice how they responded to the experience—were they careful, fearful, excited, adventurous? Talk to them about how it felt to move through the tree and what it felt like to be high above the ground.

Reflect on the tree-climbing experience:

DATE:

LOCATION:

PARTICIPANTS:

Participate in a race

Channel your child's pure, unbridled energy into the joy of participating in a race! This can be a structured community event or something less formal. And a race doesn't have to involve running. There are races for walking, swimming, and even hopping in potato sacks.

The goal isn't necessarily to win but to accomplish something and enjoy the experience of participating in the event! The important part is that they feel the exhilaration of working to reach a finish line. After the race, you can talk about winning and losing, competition, and how it felt to participate.

Write about the race:

DATE:

LOCATION:

PARTICIPANTS:

Visit a wonder of the world

The seven wonders of the ancient world were incredible architectural and sculptural achievements. Sadly, most of them have been lost to time. Only one—the Pyramids of Giza—exists today.

In contemporary times, a campaign was held to determine seven new wonders of the world: The Great Wall of China, the Mayan city of Chichén Itzá in Mexico, the ancient city of Petra in Jordan, Machu Picchu in Peru, the Christ the Redeemer statue in Rio de Janeiro, the Colosseum in Rome, and the Taj Mahal in India. All of these sites are open to visitors.

Of course, this is an aspirational experience. If travel is not possible at this time, think about what a wonder of the world would be to your family. What is a place you want your child to see? What is a sight that fills them with wonder? How can you learn more about this place?

When you've settled on a destination, dig into learning more about it through virtual tours, watching documentaries, or checking out travel guides from the library. What does your ideal itinerary look like? What interesting facts have you learned together?

Write about your travel or learning experience:

DATE:

LOCATION:

PARTICIPANTS:

Ride an elevator to the top of a tall building

To a child, an elevator can be like an amusement park ride without the lines. The shiny surfaces and mirrors, the swooshing doors. And the light-up buttons. Oh, so many buttons!

For this experience, try to find the elevator that will take you higher than any other, and take it to the highest floor you can. Let your child press the buttons (you can lift them up if they can't reach).

This is a great opportunity to discuss topics related to tall buildings, like architecture, design, and perspective. Your child might have questions, like: Does the top of a skyscraper actually scrape the sky? What are some of the tallest buildings in the world? Why are some buildings constructed to be so high?

Once you reach the highest floor possible, try to take a look outside, either through a window or from a safe balcony or rooftop patio. Talk about how things look different from this tall perch. Do the people look tiny? How far can you see? Was anything surprising?

Write about your elevator ride:

DATE:

LOCATION:

PARTICIPANTS:

BEFORE YOU'RE 5

Go whale watching

The ocean is a strange and beautiful place, and spending time on the sea is a wonderful way to teach children about this essential resource. To give children a sense of the incredible life beneath the ocean's surface, plan a whale-watching trip. Nothing inspires a sense of awe quite like seeing a whale emerge from the water. It's an exciting and thrilling adventure, it can spark a lifelong interest in ocean conservation, and it makes for a powerful family-bonding experience.

Even if you don't see a whale, other wildlife can often be spotted on a whale-watching adventure. Keep a look out for playful dolphins, beautiful marine birds, or sea turtles. And if whale watching in person isn't in the cards for you, consider watching videos of whales to introduce your child to the majestic creatures.

What happened on your whale-watching trip?

DATE:

LOCATION:

PARTICIPANTS:

Carve a pumpkin

You're in for a *gourd* time with this autumnal activity. Carving pumpkins is an excellent sensory learning experience—from choosing the perfect pumpkin (color, size, weight, texture!) to figuring out how a design will fit on the surface to scooping out the goopy seeds inside.

Once you have the pumpkin, you can sketch the design on a sheet of paper, use stencils to make carving lines on the pumpkin, or draw right on the gourd. We recommend letting your little one be in charge of art and design, while adults handle the carving. (Tip: Use a small, sharp paring knife or special pumpkin carving kit. Also keep the knife pointed away from you to avoid any mishaps.) After you've finished carving, you can separate the seeds from the slime to make baked pumpkin seeds, a delicious snack!

If carving isn't your thing, you can decorate pumpkins in many other ways. Slather it with glow-in-the-dark paint! Douse it in glue and get wild with glitter, sequins, feathers, and beads! Or maybe your pumpkin could be transformed with googly eyes, tape, or fabric?

Use the space below to jot down a few notes about the experience, and use the blank page opposite to draw your carved pumpkin.

DATE:

LOCATION:

PARTICIPANTS:

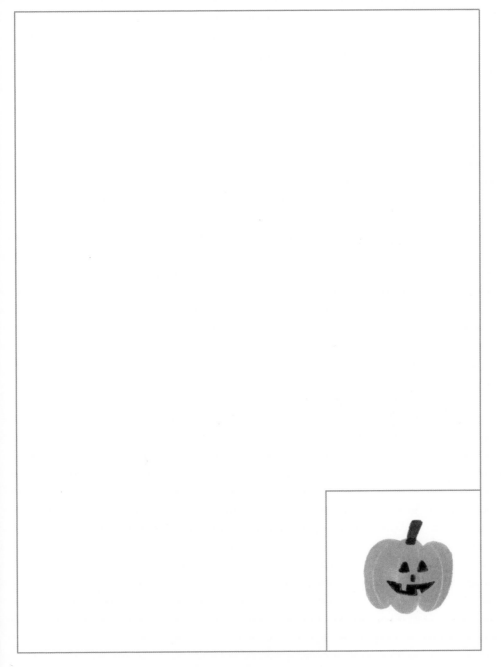

BEFORE YOU'RE 5

Sleep outside

Whether you take a nap outside on a comfy cot or blanket, or embark on a camping trip under the stars, sleeping outside establishes a connection with nature and helps children become comfortable in new environments. It's also a very memorable experience—different than falling asleep in their own beds.

The outdoors can be very calming and soothing with the natural sounds, like birds, insects, and rustling leaves, and you'll get all the benefits of fresh air.

Best of all, there are so many ways to catch some z's outside: Pitch a tent in a backyard. Spread out a blanket in a shady park. Go glamping and sleep in a yurt or safari tent.

You don't need to bring much along—the point is to get comfortable communing with nature—but don't forget items to keep your family safe and healthy, like sun block, bug repellent, flashlights, drinking water, and anything else you might need.

Write about your experience sleeping outside:

DATE:

LOCATION:

PARTICIPANTS:

Build a sandcastle

Building a sandcastle is not just a way to pass time on the beach, but it's an excellent chance for your child to express their creativity and flex their problem-solving skills!

The classic sandcastle is built with buckets of various sizes filled with damp sand. But sandcastle masterpieces can be created with no tools at all—you only need your hands, sand, and water.

Don't feel constrained by traditional castle structures, especially if you and your child want to build something else. Try sculpting animal shapes, like sea turtles or starfish. Dig a sand pit and fill it with water. Construct a tall tower (and smash it?). Or what about a making a sandman version of a snowman? Let your child's imagination run wild.

Sketch the sandcastle on the blank page opposite and jot down memories from the experience below

DATE:

LOCATION:

PARTICIPANTS:

BEFORE YOU'RE 5

Make something out of clay

Clay sculpting is an opportunity for your child to bring their vivid imagination to life and create something entirely new by hand. In addition to stoking creativity, manipulating clay helps develop small and large muscles.

Small children can squish, squeeze, pull, and roll the clay for a fun sensory experience, while older tykes can experience making three-dimensional art. You can use clay tools (like rolling pins, cookie cutters, stamps, or molds), make use of found objects (sticks, leaves, rocks), or allow your child to build freeform. Place the clay in front of them and see what they can dream up.

Use the space below to jot down a few notes about the experience, and use the blank page opposite to sketch your clay creation.

DATE:

LOCATION:

PARTICIPANTS:

BEFORE YOU'RE 5

Ride a train

Trains possess a certain magical quality. They are the vehicles of many storybooks and pieces of history that still chug along today. Step inside a train, sit down on a plush seat, and when the door opens, *poof*! You've been transported to a different place.

During a train ride, very young children can take note of the sensory experience. Point out how you can feel the rumble beneath your feet as the train moves along the tracks. Look outside and watch the landscape slide past. Listen for the whistles and toots. With an older child, discuss the interconnectivity of the cars, the predictable motion on the track, and the purpose trains serve.

If you aren't able to ride a train, visit a train station and watch and listen as the cars come and go.

Write about your experience on a train:

DATE:

LOCATION:

PARTICIPANTS:

Keep the adventures going!

Use the following pages to keep lists of places you'd like to visit, experiences you'd like to share as a family, and any other family-fun activities to inspire future adventuring.

BEFORE YOU'RE 5

50 THINGS TO DO

Draw your adventures!

Use the following blank pages to sketch things you find or create on your adventures!

BEFORE YOU'RE 5

50 THINGS TO DO

BEFORE YOU'RE 5

50 THINGS TO DO

BEFORE YOU'RE 5

50 THINGS TO DO

BEFORE YOU'RE 5